PIANO SOLO

POPULAR PIANO COVERS

ARRANGED BY THE THEORIST

Photo courtesy of Henderson Nguyen

ISBN 978-1-4950-9355-5

7777 W. BLUEMOUND RD. P.O. BOX 13819 MILWAUKEE, WI 53213

Visit Hal Leonard Online at
www.halleonard.com

HENDERSON NGUYEN, better known as The Theorist, is a Canadian composer, pianist, and songwriter. He began studying classical piano at the age of five and by age 17 had completed the requirements for the Associate of the Royal Conservatory (ARCT) diploma. He continued his studies at McMaster University, specializing in Music Education and Music Theory. Henderson subsequently spent a year at Metalworks Institute, where he completed his Audio Production/Engineering Diploma – taking courses in audio post production, sound design, and all aspects of Pro Tools.

Henderson's amazing YouTube journey began as a hobby in 2011. With his ability to play requests from his friends by ear, he saw it as an opportunity to create new arrangements and to produce videos to post online. Uploading monthly productions onto YouTube, he built a fan base all across the world, logging a massive audience of 300,000+ subscribers and over 30 million YouTube views across several years.

Live performances have taken Henderson all over the world, both as a solo artist and with PartyNext-Door, playing at such notable events as the Wireless Festival in London, Drake's OVO Festival, and Drake's Fader Fort Showcase at South by Southwest. On the production side, he has collaborated with Grammy Award-winning producers Doc McKinney and Illangelo, and artists including PartyNextDoor, JMSN, and other notable acts across different styles and genres. With these diverse experiences, Henderson has established himself as a multi-talented musician.

ALL OF ME

Words and Music by JOHN STEPHENS
and TOBY GAD
Arranged by The Theorist

Allegro cantibile ($\quarternote$ = 126)

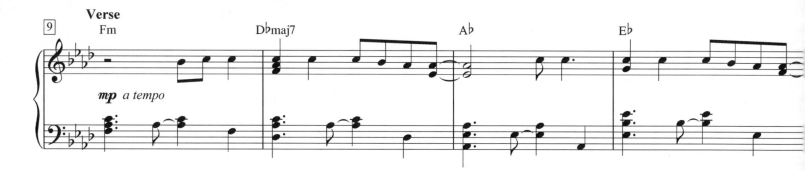

ALL OF THE LIGHTS

Words and Music by JEFFREY BHASKER,
KANYE WEST, STACY FERGUSON,
MALIK JONES, SCOTT MESCUDI
and WARREN TROTTER
Arranged by The Theorist

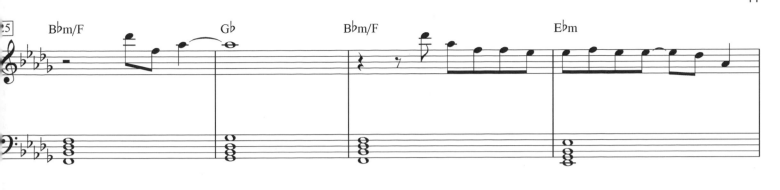

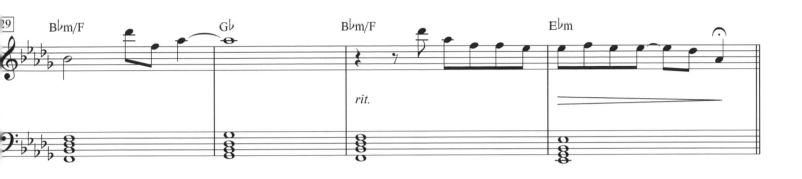

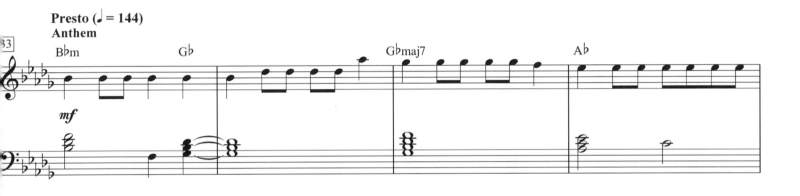

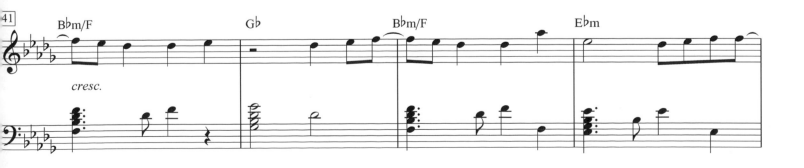

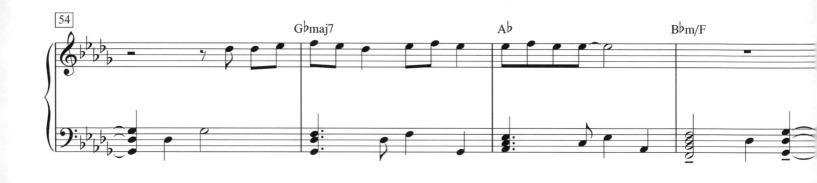

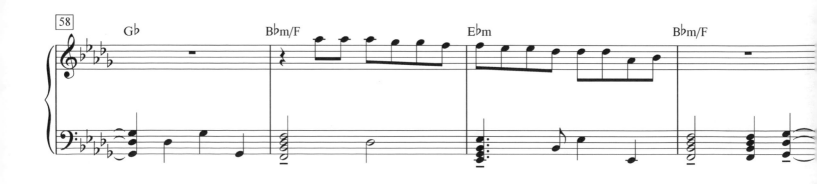

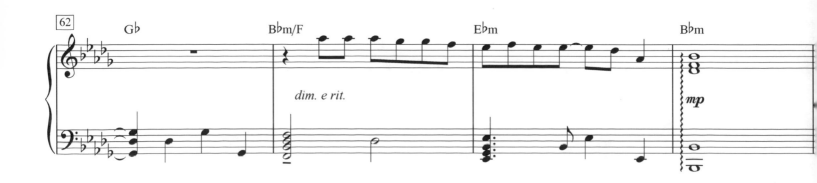

FAKE LOVE

Words and Music by AUBREY GRAHAM,
ADAM KING FEENEY, ANDERSON HERNANDEZ,
BRITTANY HAZZARD, LEON HUFF,
GENE McFADDEN and JOHN WHITEHEAD
Arranged by The Theorist

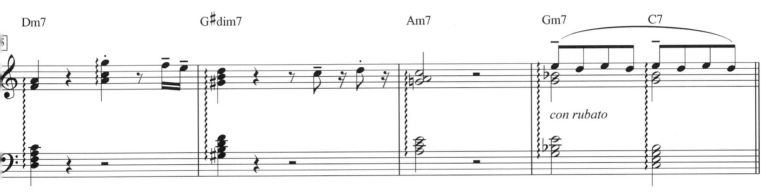

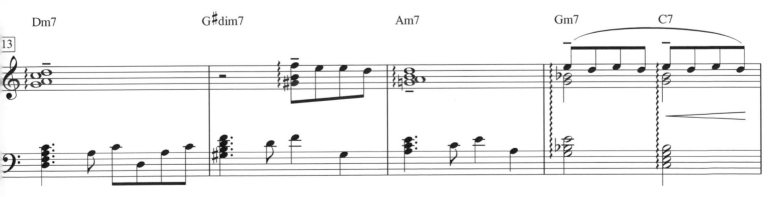

CRAZY IN LOVE
(2014 Remix)
from FIFTY SHADES OF GREY

Words and Music by BEYONCÉ KNOWLES,
RICH HARRISON, SEAN CARTER
and EUGENE RECORD
Arranged by The Theorist

EARNED IT
(Fifty Shades of Grey)
from FIFTY SHADES OF GREY

Words and Music by ABEL TESFAYE,
AHMAD BALSHE, STEPHAN MOCCIO
and JASON QUENNEVILLE
Arranged by The Theorist

FADED

Words and Music by ANDERS FROEN
GUNNAR GREVE, JESPER BORGEN
and ALAN WALKE
Arranged by The Theori

I DON'T WANNA LIVE FOREVER

(Fifty Shades Darker)

from FIFTY SHADES DARKER

Words and Music by TAYLOR SWIFT,
JACK ANTONOFF and SAM DEW
Arranged by The Theori

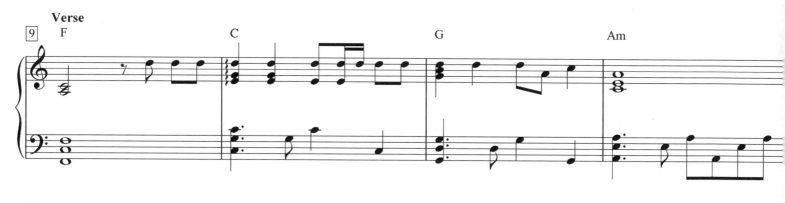

LAY ME DOWN

Words and Music by SAM SMITH,
JAMES NAPIER and ELVIN SMITH
Arranged by The Theorist

LET ME LOVE YOU

Words and Music by JUSTIN BIEBER, CARL ROSE
WILLIAM GRIGAHCINE, EDWIN PEREZ, TEDDY MENDE
ANDREW WOTMAN, ALEXANDRA TAMPOSI, LOUIS BEL
LUMIDEE CEDENO, BRIAN LEE and STEVEN MARSDE
Arranged by The Theori

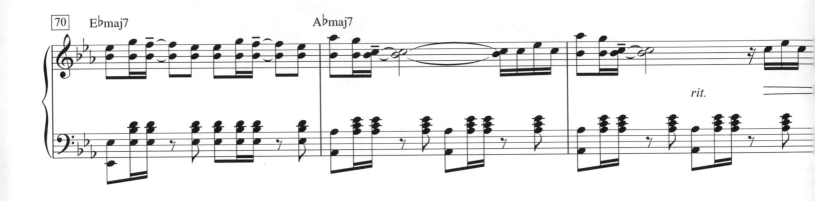

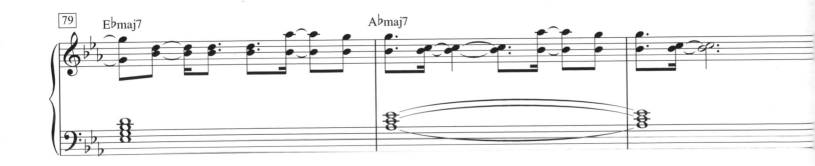

LOVE NEVER FELT SO GOOD

Words and Music by MICHAEL JACKSON
and PAUL ANKA

Allegro (♩ = 126)

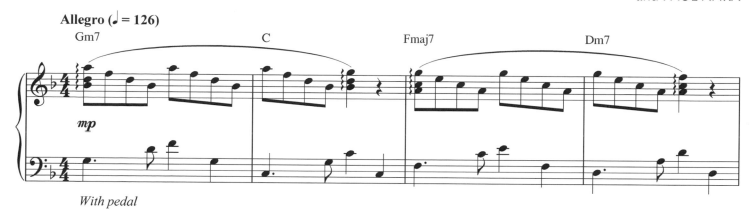

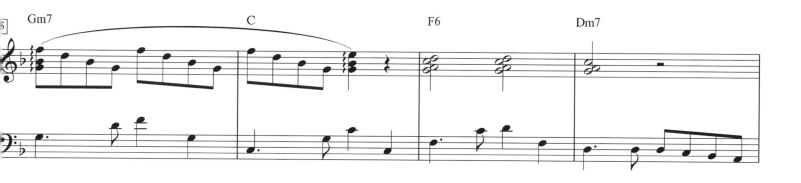

LOVE ME LIKE YOU DO

from FIFTY SHADES OF GREY

Words and Music by MAX MARTIN,
SAVAN KOTECHA, ILYA,
ALI PAYAMI and TOVE LO
Arranged by The Theorist

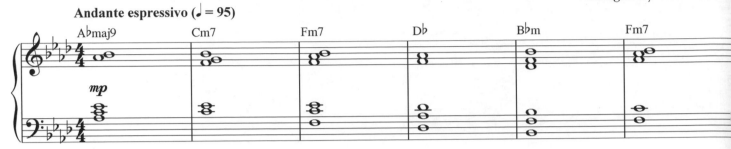

SHAPE OF YOU

Words and Music by ED SHEERAN,
KEVIN BRIGGS, KANDI BURRUSS,
TAMEKA COTTLE, STEVE MAC
and JOHN McDAID
Arranged by The Theorist

SKINNY LOVE

Words and Music by
JUSTIN VERNON
Arranged by The Theorist

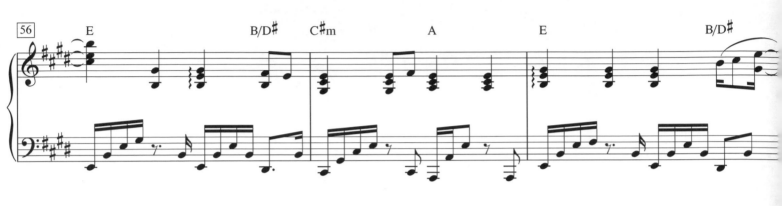

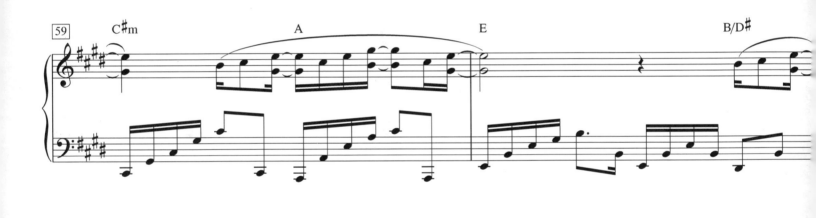

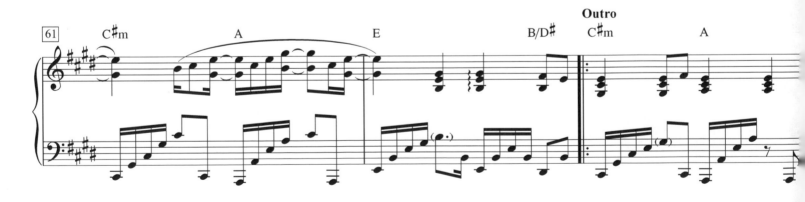

THINKING OUT LOUD

Words and Music by ED SHEERAN
and AMY WADGE
Arranged by The Theorist

THINKIN' 'BOUT YOU

Words and Music by FRANK OCEAN
and SHEA TAYLOR
Arranged by The Theorist

Allegro cantible (♩ = 128)

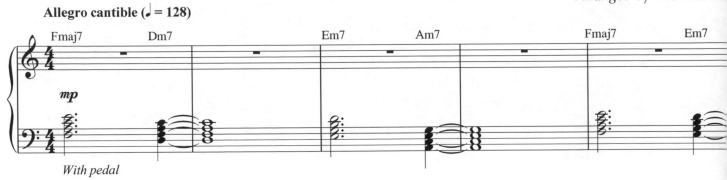

With pedal

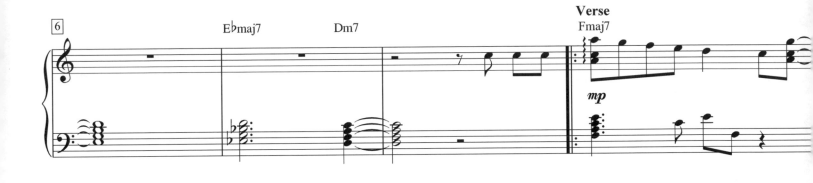

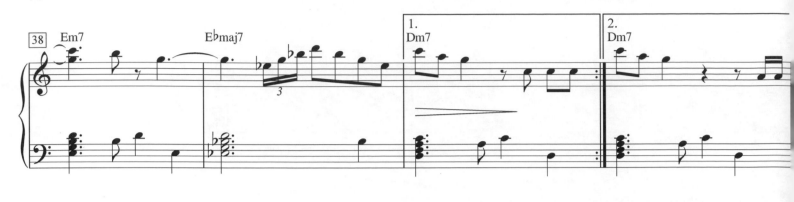

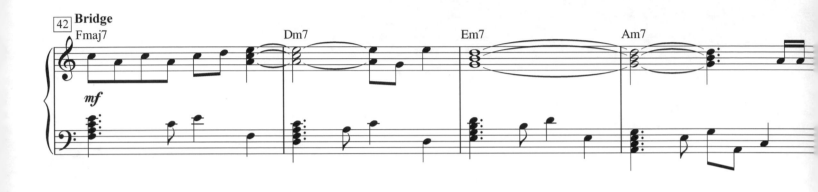

YOUNG AND BEAUTIFUL

Words and Music by RICK NOWELS
and ELIZABETH GRANT
Arranged by The Theorist

VERSACE ON THE FLOOR

Words and Music by BRUNO MARS,
PHILIP LAWRENCE, JAMES FAUNTLEROY
and CHRISTOPHER BRODY BROWN
Arranged by The Theorist